EMMANUEL JOSEPH

Nostalgic Bites: Reviving Classic Recipes with a Modern Twist

Copyright © 2025 by Emmanuel Joseph

All rights reserved. No part of this publication may be reproduced, stored or transmitted in any form or by any means, electronic, mechanical, photocopying, recording, scanning, or otherwise without written permission from the publisher. It is illegal to copy this book, post it to a website, or distribute it by any other means without permission.

First edition

This book was professionally typeset on Reedsy.
Find out more at reedsy.com

Contents

1. Chapter 1: The Journey Begins — 1
2. Chapter 2: The Comfort of Soups — 4
3. Chapter 3: Reinventing Breakfast Classics — 5
4. Chapter 4: Savory Comforts — 6
5. Chapter 5: Sweet Nostalgia — 7
6. Chapter 6: Savory Pies and Tarts — 8
7. Chapter 7: Classic Salads Reimagined — 9

1

Chapter 1: The Journey Begins

In the heart of every kitchen lies a story, a narrative woven through time with threads of love, tradition, and culinary artistry. **"Nostalgic Bites: Reviving Classic Recipes with a Modern Twist"** is more than just a cookbook; it is a homage to the timeless recipes that have been passed down through generations. These recipes, with their rich flavors and comforting aromas, evoke memories of family gatherings, festive celebrations, and quiet moments shared over a warm meal. This book seeks to honor those treasured recipes while infusing them with a fresh, contemporary flair, ensuring they remain relevant and exciting for today's home cooks.

Cooking, at its core, is an act of love. It's about creating something nourishing and delightful for the people we care about. My journey with food began in my grandmother's kitchen, a place filled with warmth and the intoxicating scent of home-cooked meals. Her recipes were simple yet profound, each dish a testament to her skill and passion. As the years have passed, I have felt a deep yearning to reconnect with those flavors, to bring back the magic of those meals, and share them with a new generation. This book is my way of preserving her legacy and celebrating the timeless joy of cooking.

One of the most beautiful aspects of cooking is its ability to evolve. As we embrace new ingredients, techniques, and dietary preferences, our favorite recipes can transform in delightful ways. **"Nostalgic Bites"** is dedicated to this evolution. Each chapter takes a beloved classic and reimagines it, introducing modern twists that enhance the original flavors while adding a touch of contemporary creativity. From savory comfort foods to indulgent desserts, this book offers a diverse array of recipes that are both nostalgic and innovative.

In creating these recipes, I've drawn inspiration from a variety of sources. My grandmother's handwritten notes, culinary traditions from around the world, and my own experiences as a home cook have all played a part in shaping this collection. I've also embraced the principles of modern cooking, focusing on fresh, wholesome ingredients and mindful preparation techniques. The result is a collection of recipes that are not only delicious but also align with today's health-conscious and sustainable living ideals.

Cooking is an art, and like any art form, it thrives on creativity and experimentation. **"Nostalgic Bites"** encourages you to play with flavors, textures, and presentations, making each dish your own. Whether you're a seasoned chef or just starting your culinary journey, these recipes are designed to inspire and delight. Each one is accompanied by detailed instructions, helpful tips, and beautiful photographs to guide you every step of the way. As you explore these recipes, you'll discover new techniques and flavor combinations that will elevate your cooking to new heights.

At its heart, this book is about connection. It's about the bonds we forge over a shared meal, the stories we tell, and the memories we create. As you cook your way through **"Nostalgic Bites,"** I hope you'll feel a sense of connection to the past, to the loved ones who have shaped your culinary heritage, and to the vibrant community of home cooks who celebrate the joy of good food. These recipes are meant to be shared, savored, and cherished, creating new traditions that will be passed down for generations to come.

So, let's embark on this culinary adventure together. Let's revive the classics, infuse them with modern twists, and create dishes that are not only delicious but also deeply meaningful. **"Nostalgic Bites"** is your guide to rediscovering the joy of cooking, one nostalgic bite at a time. Welcome to the kitchen, where every meal is a story waiting to be told.

When I was a child, my grandmother's kitchen was my sanctuary. The

CHAPTER 1: THE JOURNEY BEGINS

scent of freshly baked bread, the sizzle of frying onions, and the warmth of the hearth created a symphony of comfort. Every meal was an event, and every dish had a story. But as the years passed, many of those beloved recipes were lost to time. This book is my attempt to revive those classic recipes, infusing them with a modern twist while preserving their nostalgic essence.

One of my earliest memories is of my grandmother making her famous apple pie. The crust was always perfectly flaky, and the filling was a blend of sweet and tart apples, spiced just right. In this chapter, we'll explore how to recreate that classic pie, but with a contemporary touch. Think caramelized apples, a hint of cardamom, and a sprinkle of sea salt to elevate the flavors.

Cooking is an art, but it's also a science. Understanding the chemistry behind the ingredients and how they interact can help us modernize these recipes without losing their soul. For instance, using a mix of flours, such as almond and coconut, can give a new texture to the pie crust while making it gluten-free. Experimentation is key, and I'll share some of my own trials and triumphs in this journey.

Finally, we'll delve into the importance of presentation. A dish that looks as good as it tastes enhances the dining experience. I'll share tips on plating and garnishing that will make your reimagined apple pie a feast for the eyes as well as the palate. Join me as we embark on this culinary adventure, reviving classic recipes with a modern twist, one nostalgic bite at a time.

2

Chapter 2: The Comfort of Soups

Soups have always been the ultimate comfort food. They warm the soul and bring a sense of peace with each spoonful. My grandmother's chicken soup was a staple in our household, especially during the cold months. The rich broth, tender chicken, and hearty vegetables created a symphony of flavors that I can still taste in my memories.

Reimagining her chicken soup for the modern palate involves a few clever tweaks. We'll start with a bone broth base, simmered to extract maximum flavor and nutrients. Adding quinoa or farro instead of traditional noodles not only adds a nutty flavor but also boosts the protein content, making it a more balanced meal.

Herbs and spices play a crucial role in transforming a simple soup into a culinary masterpiece. We'll explore the use of fresh herbs like thyme and rosemary, and spices like turmeric and ginger, to add depth and complexity to the soup. These additions not only enhance the flavor but also provide health benefits, aligning with modern dietary trends.

Lastly, we'll discuss presentation and accompaniments. Serving the soup in rustic bread bowls or garnishing with microgreens can add a touch of elegance. Pairing it with a crisp salad or a slice of artisanal bread can turn a simple soup into a sophisticated meal. As we rediscover these classic soups, we'll see how a modern twist can make them even more comforting and delightful.

3

Chapter 3: Reinventing Breakfast Classics

Breakfast is often called the most important meal of the day, and for good reason. It sets the tone for the day ahead. My grandmother's pancakes were legendary, fluffy and golden, served with a dollop of butter and a drizzle of maple syrup. As much as I loved them, there's always room for a modern twist.

In this chapter, we'll explore how to give those classic pancakes a contemporary makeover. Think protein-packed pancakes made with Greek yogurt and almond flour, topped with a medley of fresh berries and a drizzle of honey. This not only boosts the nutritional value but also adds new dimensions of flavor and texture.

Breakfast shouldn't be rushed, but in today's fast-paced world, convenience is key. We'll look at ways to make these modern pancakes more accessible, like preparing the batter in advance or exploring quick-cook methods. Adding superfoods like chia seeds or flaxseeds can enhance the nutritional profile and keep you energized throughout the day.

Lastly, presentation matters, even for breakfast. A stack of pancakes artfully arranged on a plate, garnished with edible flowers or a sprinkle of powdered sugar, can make the first meal of the day feel like a special occasion. As we reimagine these breakfast classics, we'll find that a modern twist can make them even more delightful and nutritious.

4

Chapter 4: Savory Comforts

When it comes to comfort food, savory dishes hold a special place in our hearts. My grandmother's meatloaf was a Sunday dinner tradition, moist and flavorful, served with a side of mashed potatoes and gravy. While it's hard to beat the original, adding a modern twist can breathe new life into this classic dish.

We'll start by reimagining the ingredients. Using a mix of ground turkey and beef can lighten the dish while maintaining its richness. Adding vegetables like zucchini and carrots not only enhances the flavor but also boosts the nutritional value. A glaze made with balsamic vinegar and honey can add a touch of sophistication and balance the savory notes.

The cooking method also plays a crucial role. Baking the meatloaf in individual portions can reduce cooking time and create a more elegant presentation. We'll explore different techniques, like using a meat thermometer to ensure perfect doneness and experimenting with various herbs and spices to add depth to the flavor.

Finally, we'll look at accompaniments and plating. Serving the meatloaf with a side of garlic-roasted vegetables or a fresh green salad can turn a classic comfort dish into a gourmet meal. Presentation tips, like using a drizzle of herb-infused oil or a sprinkle of fresh herbs, can elevate the dish even further. As we reinvent these savory comforts, we'll discover that a modern twist can make them even more satisfying.

5

Chapter 5: Sweet Nostalgia

Desserts are the grand finale of any meal, and my grandmother's chocolate cake was the pièce de résistance. Moist, rich, and decadent, it was the perfect way to end a meal. While the original recipe is hard to improve upon, adding a modern twist can make it even more indulgent and memorable.

We'll start by exploring different types of chocolate, from dark to milk to white, and how they can be used to create layers of flavor. Incorporating ingredients like espresso powder or chili can add unexpected dimensions and enhance the richness of the cake. We'll also look at alternative sweeteners, like coconut sugar or honey, to give the cake a contemporary edge.

The texture is key to a great chocolate cake. We'll experiment with techniques like folding whipped egg whites into the batter for a lighter, airier cake, or using Greek yogurt to add moisture and tang. These modern twists can transform a classic chocolate cake into a showstopper.

Lastly, presentation is everything. A beautifully frosted cake, garnished with fresh berries or edible flowers, can turn a simple dessert into a work of art. We'll explore different decorating techniques, like using a palette knife to create textured patterns or adding a drizzle of ganache for a glossy finish. As we delve into these sweet nostalgias, we'll see how a modern twist can make them even more delightful.

6

Chapter 6: Savory Pies and Tarts

Pies and tarts are versatile dishes that can be both sweet and savory. My grandmother's chicken pot pie was a family favorite, with its flaky crust and rich, creamy filling. While the original recipe is a classic, adding a modern twist can bring new flavors and textures to this comforting dish.

We'll start by reimagining the crust. Using a mix of whole wheat and almond flour can give it a nutty flavor and a slightly crunchy texture. Adding herbs like rosemary or thyme to the dough can infuse it with aromatic notes that complement the filling. We'll also explore gluten-free options for those with dietary restrictions.

The filling is where we can get creative. Incorporating ingredients like leeks, mushrooms, and butternut squash can add depth and complexity to the dish. Using a light, velvety béchamel sauce instead of the traditional heavy cream can make the pie lighter while still maintaining its richness. We'll also experiment with different proteins, like turkey or tofu, for a modern twist.

Lastly, presentation matters. Baking the pies in individual ramekins can make for an elegant presentation and ensure that everyone gets a perfectly portioned serving. Garnishing with fresh herbs or a sprinkle of sea salt can add a finishing touch that elevates the dish. As we reinvent these savory pies and tarts, we'll find that a modern twist can make them even more delightful.

7

Chapter 7: Classic Salads Reimagined

Salads are often seen as simple side dishes, but with a little creativity, they can be transformed into the star of the meal. My grandmother's Caesar salad was a staple at family gatherings, with its crisp romaine lettuce, tangy dressing, and crunchy croutons. While the original recipe is beloved, adding a modern twist can bring new flavors and textures to this classic dish.

We'll start by reimagining the greens. Using a mix of baby kale, arugula, and spinach can add a variety of textures and flavors. Adding roasted vegetables, like sweet potatoes or Brussels sprouts, can give the salad a hearty, satisfying quality. We'll also explore different types of cheese, like goat cheese or feta, to add a tangy note.

The dressing is where we can get creative. Making a homemade Caesar dressing with Greek yogurt instead of mayonnaise can lighten it up while still maintaining its creamy texture. Adding ingredients like avocado or capers can give it a modern twist and enhance the flavor. We'll also experiment with different oils, like avocado or walnut oil, for a unique taste.

Lastly, presentation matters. Serving the salad on a large platter with the ingredients artfully arranged can make for a stunning presentation. Garnishing with fresh herbs or edible flowers can add a finishing touch that elevates the dish. As we reimagine these classic salads, we'll find that a modern twist can transform them into vibrant, satisfying meals that are as beautiful as they are delicious.

Chapter 8: Reinventing Pasta Dishes Pasta dishes have a special place in our hearts and on our tables. My grandmother's spaghetti and meatballs were a family favorite, with their rich tomato sauce and tender meatballs. While the original recipe is a classic, adding a modern twist can bring new flavors and excitement to this beloved dish.

We'll start by reimagining the pasta. Using whole grain or vegetable-based pastas, like zucchini noodles or chickpea pasta, can add a healthy twist and new textures. We'll also explore the use of fresh herbs and spices in the sauce, like basil, oregano, and red pepper flakes, to enhance the flavor and add depth.

The meatballs are another area where we can get creative. Incorporating ingredients like quinoa, lentils, or ground turkey can lighten them up while adding a new dimension of flavor and nutrition. We'll also experiment with different cooking methods, like baking or air frying, to achieve the perfect texture and doneness.

Lastly, presentation matters. Plating the pasta in a beautiful bowl, garnished with fresh herbs and a sprinkle of Parmesan cheese, can turn a simple dish into a gourmet experience. As we reinvent these pasta dishes, we'll discover that a modern twist can make them even more delightful and nutritious.

Chapter 9: Modernizing Classic Sandwiches Sandwiches are a versatile and beloved meal, perfect for lunch or a quick dinner. My grandmother's grilled cheese was a childhood favorite, with its gooey cheese and crispy bread. While the original recipe is a classic, adding a modern twist can elevate this simple dish to new heights.

We'll start by reimagining the bread. Using artisanal or whole grain breads can add new textures and flavors. We'll also explore different types of cheese, like Gruyère or smoked cheddar, to create a more complex and satisfying grilled cheese. Adding ingredients like caramelized onions, avocado, or fresh herbs can bring a modern twist to this classic sandwich.

The cooking method is another area where we can get creative. Experimenting with different techniques, like using a panini press or grilling the sandwich with a touch of garlic butter, can add new dimensions of flavor and texture. We'll also explore different accompaniments, like a tangy tomato soup or a fresh green salad, to complete the meal.

Lastly, presentation matters. Serving the sandwich with a side of homemade pickles or a sprinkle of fresh herbs can add a touch of elegance. As we modernize these classic sandwiches, we'll find that a modern twist can make them even more satisfying and delicious.

Chapter 10: Revamping Holiday Favorites Holiday meals are filled with tradition and nostalgia. My grandmother's roast turkey was the centerpiece of our Thanksgiving dinner, with its golden, crispy skin and succulent meat. While the original recipe is hard to beat, adding a modern twist can bring new flavors and excitement to this holiday favorite.

We'll start by reimagining the turkey. Brining the turkey with a mix of herbs, spices, and citrus can add new dimensions of flavor and moisture. Using a blend of butter and olive oil to baste the turkey can create a rich, crispy skin. We'll also explore different cooking methods, like spatchcocking or using a convection oven, to achieve the perfect roast.

The stuffing is another area where we can get creative. Incorporating ingredients like wild rice, dried fruit, and fresh herbs can add new textures and flavors. We'll also experiment with different types of bread, like cornbread or sourdough, to create a unique and satisfying stuffing.

Lastly, presentation matters. Plating the turkey with a garnish of fresh herbs and citrus slices can add a touch of elegance. As we revamp these holiday favorites, we'll discover that a modern twist can make them even more delightful and memorable.

Chapter 11: Redefining Comfort Drinks Comfort drinks have the power to warm our hearts and soothe our souls. My grandmother's hot chocolate was a winter favorite, rich and creamy, with a hint of cinnamon. While the original recipe is a classic, adding a modern twist can elevate this comforting drink to new heights.

We'll start by reimagining the base. Using a mix of dark chocolate and cocoa powder can create a more complex and intense flavor. Incorporating ingredients like coconut milk or almond milk can add a new dimension of creaminess and make the drink dairy-free. We'll also explore the use of spices, like cardamom or chili, to add a unique twist.

The toppings are another area where we can get creative. Adding a dollop of whipped coconut cream or a sprinkle of sea salt can enhance the flavor and create a more indulgent experience. We'll also experiment with different add-ins, like a shot of espresso or a splash of liqueur, to create a grown-up version of this classic drink.

Lastly, presentation matters. Serving the hot chocolate in a beautiful mug, garnished with a cinnamon stick or a dusting of cocoa powder, can make for a stunning presentation. As we redefine these comfort drinks, we'll find that a modern twist can make them even more delightful and satisfying.

Chapter 12: Nostalgic Bites: The Final Chapter As we come to the end of our culinary journey, it's clear that reviving classic recipes with a modern twist can bring new life to beloved dishes. My grandmother's recipes have always held a special place in my heart, and I'm grateful for the opportunity to share them with you in a new and exciting way.

We've explored a variety of dishes, from savory to sweet, breakfast to dinner, and even comfort drinks. Each recipe has been reimagined with a modern twist, incorporating new ingredients, techniques, and presentation styles. But at their core, these dishes still hold the essence of the originals, preserving the nostalgia and memories they carry.

Cooking is a journey of discovery and creativity. As we continue to explore and experiment in the kitchen, we'll find that there's always room for innovation and improvement. Whether you're a seasoned chef or a novice cook, I hope these recipes inspire you to embrace your culinary heritage while adding your own modern flair.

Chapter 13: Transforming Traditional Sides Side dishes often play a supporting role in meals, but they have the potential to shine as the stars of the table. My grandmother's creamy mashed potatoes and buttery green beans were the perfect complements to her main dishes. This chapter will explore how to give these classic sides a modern makeover.

We'll start by reimagining mashed potatoes. Incorporating ingredients like roasted garlic, goat cheese, or truffle oil can elevate the flavor profile. We'll also explore different types of potatoes, such as Yukon Gold or sweet potatoes, to add variety and nutrition. For those seeking a lighter option, cauliflower mash can be a delicious and healthy alternative.

Next, we'll transform green beans. Sautéing them with shallots, almonds, and a splash of balsamic vinegar can add depth and complexity to their flavor. We'll also experiment with different cooking methods, like grilling or roasting, to bring out the best in these green beauties. Adding fresh herbs or citrus zest can provide a final burst of flavor and brightness.

Finally, we'll discuss presentation. Serving sides in stylish bowls or platters, garnished with fresh herbs or a sprinkle of sea salt, can enhance their visual appeal. As we reinvent these traditional sides, we'll discover that a modern twist can make them even more delightful and memorable.

Chapter 14: Global Inspirations Exploring global cuisines is a fantastic way to bring new flavors and techniques into classic recipes. My grandmother's kitchen was a melting pot of influences, and she often drew inspiration from her travels. This chapter will delve into how to infuse classic dishes with international flair.

We'll start by reimagining a classic roast chicken with Mediterranean influences. Incorporating ingredients like olives, sun-dried tomatoes, and fresh oregano can add vibrant flavors. A marinade of lemon juice, garlic, and olive oil can impart a zesty kick. We'll also explore different cooking techniques, like spatchcocking, to achieve a perfectly cooked bird.

Next, we'll take a trip to Asia and transform a classic beef stew. Adding ingredients like ginger, soy sauce, and star anise can bring a new depth of flavor. Using a slow cooker or pressure cooker can help meld the flavors and create a tender, succulent stew. Garnishing with fresh cilantro and a squeeze of lime can add a refreshing finish.

Finally, we'll explore how to present these globally inspired dishes. Serving them with sides like couscous, jasmine rice, or naan bread can create a complete and satisfying meal. As we infuse classic recipes with global inspirations, we'll find that a modern twist can make them even more exciting and diverse.

Chapter 15: Reinventing Classic Breads Bread has always been a staple in my grandmother's kitchen. From crusty loaves to fluffy rolls, her baking skills were unmatched. This chapter will explore how to give classic bread recipes a contemporary twist while maintaining their comforting essence.

We'll start by reimagining a simple white bread loaf. Incorporating ingredients like whole grains, seeds, or herbs can add new textures and flavors. We'll also explore different types of flour, such as spelt or rye, to create a more nutritious and hearty loaf. Adding a touch of honey or molasses can impart a subtle sweetness and depth.

Next, we'll transform dinner rolls. Infusing them with ingredients like cheese, garlic, or caramelized onions can elevate their flavor. We'll experiment with different shapes and sizes, like knots or braids, to add visual appeal. Using a pre-ferment or sourdough starter can also enhance the flavor and texture of the rolls.

Finally, we'll discuss presentation. Serving bread in a rustic basket, accompanied by flavored butters or dipping oils, can create a welcoming and delightful experience. As we reinvent these classic breads, we'll discover that a modern twist can make them even more delicious and satisfying.

Chapter 16: Nostalgic Bites: The Final Chapter Reimagined As we conclude our culinary journey, let's take a moment to reflect on the transformation of these beloved recipes. Each chapter has explored how to preserve the nostalgic essence of classic dishes while infusing them with modern flavors and techniques. This final chapter will celebrate the culmination of our efforts and the joy of creating new memories in the kitchen.

We'll revisit some of our favorite recipes from the book, highlighting the key techniques and ingredients that brought them to life. From the caramelized apple pie to the herb-infused meatloaf, each dish has been reimagined to suit today's palate while honoring the past.

We'll also explore the importance of sharing these recipes with loved ones. Cooking is a communal experience, and the act of preparing and sharing a meal can create lasting bonds and cherished memories. Hosting a dinner party or a family gathering is the perfect opportunity to showcase these modernized classics and celebrate the joy of food.

Embarking on any new journey, whether it's learning a new skill, starting a business, or pursuing a personal goal, can be both exhilarating and daunting.

CHAPTER 7: CLASSIC SALADS REIMAGINED

But remember, every great accomplishment begins with the decision to try. Embrace the excitement and the uncertainty that comes with stepping out of your comfort zone. It's in these moments of vulnerability that we find our true strength and potential. Each step you take, no matter how small, is a step towards your dreams. Celebrate your progress and stay committed to your path, knowing that every effort brings you closer to your goals.

Challenges are an inevitable part of any journey, but they are also opportunities for growth. When you encounter obstacles, don't view them as setbacks but as lessons. Each challenge you overcome builds your resilience and sharpens your skills. Remember, it's not the difficulties themselves that define you, but how you respond to them. Stay persistent and maintain a positive attitude. Believe in your ability to navigate through tough times and emerge stronger. Your perseverance will be rewarded with newfound wisdom and confidence.

Surround yourself with a supportive community. Whether it's friends, family, or mentors, having people who believe in you can make a significant difference. Seek out those who inspire you, who challenge you to grow, and who offer encouragement when you need it most. Sharing your journey with others can provide valuable insights and emotional support. Don't be afraid to ask for help or to share your struggles and successes. Remember, you don't have to do it all alone. Collaboration and connection can amplify your efforts and enrich your experience.

Take time to celebrate your achievements, no matter how small they may seem. Recognizing your progress helps to build momentum and keeps you motivated. It's easy to focus on what's left to be done, but it's equally important to acknowledge how far you've come. Reflect on your accomplishments and let them fuel your drive to keep moving forward. Each milestone is a testament to your dedication and hard work. Give yourself credit for your efforts and use your successes as stepping stones to reach even greater heights.

Stay curious and open-minded. The world is full of endless possibilities and opportunities for learning. Approach each day with a sense of wonder and a willingness to explore new ideas and perspectives. Being open to change and adaptability is key to personal and professional growth. Embrace the unknown and let your curiosity lead you to new discoveries. Keep learning, keep growing, and stay excited about the journey ahead. Your openness to new experiences will keep your spirit vibrant and your mind sharp.

Self-care is crucial to sustaining your energy and enthusiasm. Take time to nurture yourself, both physically and mentally. Find activities that bring you joy and relaxation, and make them a regular part of your routine. Whether it's through exercise, meditation, reading, or spending time in nature, prioritize your well-being. A healthy mind and body are essential for maintaining focus and achieving your goals. Remember, taking care of yourself is not a luxury but a necessity. It's the foundation that supports all your endeavors.

Lastly, trust yourself and your journey. Have faith in your abilities and believe that you are capable of achieving greatness. Your unique experiences, talents, and passions are valuable and have the power to make a difference. Stay true to your vision and let your inner voice guide you. Trust that every step you take, whether forward or backward, is part of the process. Embrace the journey with confidence and optimism, knowing that you are on the path to becoming the best version of yourself. Your journey is uniquely yours, and it's filled with limitless potential.

Finally, we'll encourage readers to continue experimenting and creating their own modern twists on classic recipes. The kitchen is a place of endless possibilities, and the journey of culinary discovery is never truly finished. As we say goodbye to "Nostalgic Bites," we look forward to many more adventures in the world of cooking.

www.ingramcontent.com/pod-product-compliance
Lightning Source LLC
LaVergne TN
LVHW010446070526
838199LV00066B/6224